A Garland Series

The English Stage
Attack and Defense 1577 - 1730

A collection of 90 important works
reprinted in photo-facsimile in 50 volumes

edited by
Arthur Freeman
Boston University

Animadversions on Mr. Congreve's Late Answer to Mr. Collier

with a preface
for the Garland Edition by

Arthur Freeman

Garland Publishing, Inc., New York & London

1972

Library of Congress Cataloging in Publication Data
Main entry under title:

Animadversions on Mr. Congreve's late answer to
    Mr. Collier.

    (The English stage: attack and defense, 1577-1730)
    Attributed to George Powell. Cf. Pref.
    Reprint of the 1698 ed.
    "Wing A3195."
    1. Congreve, William, 1670-1729. Amendments upon
Mr. Collier's false and imperfect citations.
2. Theater--Moral and religious aspects. 3. Theater
--England. I. Powell, George, 1658?-1714. II. Title.
III. Series.
PN2047.C62C623 1972   792'.013   78-170440
ISBN 0-8240-0607-0

Preface

This dialogue, a precursor of Collier's own Defence of the Short View *and a reply to Congreve's* Amendments, *followed the latter by about two months and preceded the former by two. Hooker and Lowe-Arnott-Robinson consider it anonymous, but Edmund Gosse (*Life of Congreve, 1888) *has offered an apparently forgotten claim for the quarrelsome George Powell (?1658-1714), actor, dramatist, and enemy of Cibber, who played the part of Worthy in the original production of* The Relapse *(1697). Our reprint is prepared from an interesting copy of the first edition in the possession of the Publishers, collating $A^8 a^8 B$-$F^8 G^4$ (A1 blank). Some of the missing names have been filled in here by an early hand, and the flyleaf bears the piquant inscription "E dono Tho. Gramer [?] Sept. 18. 98" (the book was first advertised on 3-8 September) followed by "Pix. Trotter Poetesses." Now Mary Pix and Catherine Trotter Cockburn, playwrights, associates of Cibber, and protégées of Congreve were no friends of Powell,*

5

PREFACE

Mrs. Pix having recently accused him inter alia *of plagiarism from her* Deceiver Deceived, *and Powell having just acted in a nasty satire upon the two poetical ladies (and Mrs. Manley),* Female Wits. *The question of authorship remains open, of course, but George Powell certainly was capable of animadversions on the patron of his antagonists — theatrically committed though he was.*

Lowe-Arnott-Robinson 299; Hooker 15; Wing A3195.

July, 1972

A.F.

ANIMADVERSIONS

ON

Mr. Congreves

LATE

ANSWER

TO

Mr. *COLLIER,* &c.

ANIMADVERSIONS
ON
Mr. Congreve's
LATE
ANSWER
TO
Mr. *COLLIER.*
IN A

DIALOGUE between Mr. *Smith* and Mr. *Johnson.*

With the Characters of the present *POETS;*

And some Offers towards

New-Modeling the *STAGE.*

Sr. Jof. *Egad, there are good Morals to be pick'd out of* Æsop's *Fables, let me tell you that, and* Reynard the Fox *too.*

Bluff. *Damn your Morals*

Sr. Jof. *Pritbee don't speak so Loud.*

Bluff. *Damn your Morals, I must revenge the Affront done to my Honor.*

Old Batch. *Page* 47.

LONDON, Printed for *John Nutt,* near *Stationers-Hall.* 1698.

TO THE
INGENIOUS
Mr. ———.

O Could I write like D——s sternly loud,

That *Ixion* Author, in his Fancy proud

To chafe a Goddefs,—— but embrace a Cloud.

With ftretch'd out Wings on such Purfuits he
(foars,

Preffes the Cloud, and then the Thunder roars.

Loft in a Fog, he fucks Infection there:

The very *uglieft Dæmon* of the Air;

A 4

On

On whose foul Aspect should you sagely look,

You can't but fancy that he's Thunder-struck.

Such heavy Dulness dwells upon his Face,

You read him much a Critick,—more an A---.

Or cou!d I run in *Hop*----s thundring strain,

He who the *Triumphs* Sung of Peaceful Reign:

In noisy roar of Numbers to excell,

And gain to Kiss that Hand which fought so
(well.

He who had *ev'ry Muse*,——and yet had none;

With all his Grand-Sire's nonsense added to his
(own.

Or could I write like the two Female⎫
(things,⎪
With *Muse Pen-feather'd*, guiltless yet of ⎬
(Wings;⎪
And yet, it strives to Fly, and thinks it Sings.⎭

Just like the Dames themselves, who flant in
(Town,
And flutter loosely, but to tumble down.

The

The laſt that writ, of theſe preſuming two,

(For that *Queen Ca* ~~than~~ *ne* is no Play 'tis true)

And yet to Spell is more than ſhe can do,

Told a High Princeſs, ſhe from Men had torn

Thoſe *Bays.* which they had long engroſs'd and
(worn.

But when ſhe offers at our Sex thus Fair,

With four fine Copies to her Play,---O rare!

If ſhe feels Manhood ſhoot---'tis I know where.

Let them ſcrawl on, and Loll, and Wiſh at eaſe,

(A Feather oft does Woman's Fancy pleaſe.)

Till by their Muſe (more jilt than they) accurſt,

We know (if poſſible) which writes the worſt.

Beneath theſe Pictures, ſure there needs no
(name,
Nor will I give what they ne'er got in Fame.

Renown'd

Renown'd like D——y, for his written Chat

Of *Quixots*, Monkys, and we know not what.

Light in repute with all the Sacred Throng.

Unless for *heavy Burthen in a Song*.

With stutt'ring Muse, and Self, he Sings,----or
(says

He writes things sometimes, but his last were
(Plays.

Capt Vanorook

Next struts in *Foppington* of high Renown,

Call'd the *Beau-writer* by the Sparkish Town;

But him for all his Failings, I'll Excuse,

He makes fair promises to quit his Muse:

Yet here's the Danger, a *Relapse* before,

Shews that the scurvy Sickness is not o'er;

And drunken Men who know not what they do,

Reel first on one side, then on 'tother too.

Next

Next, let the needy Gil——n peep abroad,

Without a Muſe, but more without a God.

The firſt he claims, the latter's only Nam'd

In idle Talk,——— ſo to be doubly Damn'd.

Of all our throng of Wits and Men of Parts,

'Tis certain he has had his full Deſerts,

In a late Book, where of moſt Plays he treats,

Of his dear ſelf who knows what he Repeats?

He tells you how his Beads were from him
(thrown,
Then what Religion has he now? Why none.

Equal to him in Poetry and Fame,

Comes one who both has got, and loſt a Name.

Se——le

Se——*le*, who, when he gain'd a faint applause,

Play'd a Juſt *V*——*n*, ſhew'd us what he was.

He yields, no doubt, Great----! ſoon to you,

We know, his recantations are not new.

But he, 'tis fear'd is fond of *Gil*——*n*'s Curſe,

Eager of change, tho' ſtill from bad to worſe.

Yet thou haſt flaſh'd ſuch rays of Sacred Light,

Sure, their dark Souls, for once, might find
(the right.

Next in deſert ſtands one, a Man of Wit,

Made ſo by what he ſtole, not what he writ.

But ſhould each Bird pluck from this Crow
(his own.
His Plumes would all be loſt, and he undone.

In ſome Years ſpace, Play drops from thieving
(*Muſe*,
So long a time ſhe takes to pick, and chooſe.

Thus

Thus while he bears his burthens from the reſt,

His Title's but *The Aſs of Wit*, at Beſt.

Yet we may gueſs this Malefactor's end.

Tho' the old J——ohn H——opkins be now his Friend.

Inferior ev'n to theſe, *Mot--x* appear,

Do thou the laſt in Wit, bring up the Rear:

Let the next piece you write, to Damn the Pit,

Be call'd not *Beauty in Diſtreſs*, but *Wit*.

Poor ev'ry way, in Poetry and Pence,

Keep your Advice, and write, to ſhew your Senſe.

And if you can't do better for your Heart,

Think not our *Charity your own Deſert*.

But be as conſcious ſtill, you want a prop,

As when both Prieſt and Poet bore you up.

On

On each side one, but now as Matters stand;

I wonder which took place, and dear Right-hand.

    The Priest, no doubt; for Dr--en Pious grown,

Throws down his Arms and yields to you alone.

Triumphant--! o'er thy Vanquish'd Foes,

As such, I wish not now to write like those.

If 'e'er too high my rais'd Ambition flew,

It was, like thee, to Write and Conquer too.

————————————————

THE

THE

PREFACE

TO THE

READER.

CUstom has made it requi-
site, that every body
that Writes, should have something call'd a Preface prefix'd
to

to his Undertaking; but 'tis here, as in writing Private Letters, a Man has always the hardest Task, when he has no Business; so I have little else incumbent on me, but to let all my loving Friends in Town know, that I am very Well, and all that, as Mr. Bays says.

As for News, (now you may suppose me writing to a Country Friend) Dear such a one,

Because I have none else to tell you; Mr. Congreve has set out a Book in Vin-

dication

dication of his Plays from Mr. Collier's. Most of the other Scribling Sparks o'th Town, have discharg'd their little Artillery and their Spleen as well as he, but not one Breach have they made yet in Mr. Collier's Bastions; they are too well Lin'd against the disorderly Fire of such Poppers. And I am told, he will very soon make a Sally, which I am positive, will raise their Siege, and open for himself a vast Field to Triumph in, who even in his Walls was Conqueror.

a   Being

The Preface.

Being very Idle, I made bold to seize the Reins of your Friend Will's Prose Pegasus, (and yet his most fiery Poetick Steed is no better) to make my Remarks a little how he foam'd, and champ'd upon his Bit; and tho' he was a Guift Horse to the World this bout (for I think no body bought him) I presum'd to look him in the Mouth. He had many Faults, I found as I View'd him; very Headstrong; when Spurr'd, apt neither to run, nor Pace,

but

but *Kick* and *Fling*, or at best, fall into a hard uncouth, unsufferable *Trot*. I obferv'd him from *Head* to *Tail*, he was both *Crop'd* and *Bob'd*. He was fo untoward, he had given his *Rider* (while he pretended to shew him) several *Falls*, and fo I thought fit to take hold of him.

This is all the *Account* I think neceffary to be given of my *Pebble-ftone* attempt upon the very *Front* of this *Goliah*; one, who braves *Heaven* as much as

the

The Preface

the former did, even in his most Modest and Innocent Play as he calls it. I'll give you an Instance or two.---

Mourning Bride, *P.* 20. *Alm.----*How I have Mourn'd and Pray'd,

For I have Pray'd to thee as to a Saint;

A Roman-Catholick *no doubt, but on*——

And thou hast hear'd my Prayer, for thou
(art come

To my Distress, to my Despair, which
(Heav'n

Without thee cannot Cure.

This

Ozayn. Then *Garcia* shall ly Panting on
(thy Bosom,
Luxurious, Revelling amidst thy Charms,
And thou perforce must yield and Aid
(his Transports.

This is luxuriously Modest, on my Word. I wonder who yielded to Aid Mr. Congreve's Transports when writ this: He must certainly have beheld several beautiful Idea's of Lust, to draw this Picture of Obscenity by, as well as the other Painter had, who drew his Luscious Venus.

a 4 *Now*

The Preface

Now for another touch of Prophaneness——

Alm. 'Tis more than Recompence to see
(thy Face;

If Heaven is greater Joy, it is no Hap-
(pineſs,

For 'tis not to be born. ——

If that be Mr. Congreve's Opinion, he need not covet to go to Heaven at all, but to ſtay and Ogle his Dear Bra-cilla, with ſneaking looks un-der his Hat, in the little ſide Box.

One more, and then I have done; tis a moſt rampant one.

King.

King. Better for him to tempt the Rage Page 26.
(of Heaven,

And wrench the Bolt red hissing from
(the hand

Of him that Thunders, than but think
(that Insolence.

'Tis daring for a God——

*Now, he might have made
something of this with a little Paraphrase, and avoided
the Prophanity too, as thus----*

Better for him to tempt the Tavern's
(Fury,

In the full Face of a *Presenting Jury.*

Snatch

The Preface.

Snatch the brisk Glafs red fparkling from
(the hand

Of him that draws it——

     Comment. (Drawer underftand.

Than but to think to thruft out Snout
(like Hog,

Or Bark, or fo---- 'tis daring for a Dog.

*Pray now, was not our
Poet a very infolent Capa-
neus, to Brave a true Jove,
and real Thunder ? But 'tis
my Opinion, that be who no
Morality to Men, can't fhew
any Religion to a God.*

As

As an Instance of his un-Gentile Principles; One Mr. P—— shew'd him his Play, he apporv'd on't, and tho' perhaps it deserv'd its Fate, yet 'tis very well known who it was, that by his Interest of Voices, caus'd it to be damn'd. I instance this Gentleman particularly, because, his false Friend fail'd in all his other attempts of the like good Office.

However, this Gentleman's Countrymen are not much oblig'd to him; for he is pleas'd (where he confesses his Demerits) to say he hopes the Faults are to be Excus'd

in

The Preface.

shall only say, *That I think it does not deserve it.*

Others perhaps may fancy that I have been too Severe upon Mr. Congreve ; but I shall only desire these Gentlemen to take a slight View of his Book, and I dare engage they'll soon be of another Opinion. They'll find his Pages fuller of Malice than right Reasoning, and instead of being stor'd with Sense, blacken'd with Gall and Spleen. His way of Answering Mr. Collier, *is with Satyr and Reflection; and since he has*

set

to the Reader.

ſet the Copy, *he can't take it ill if he is Imitated, eſpecially when he ſees we have obſerv'd our Diſtance, and not preſum'd to cope with him in his* Maſter-piece.

For we are all aſſur'd his **Prophetick Truth's** *now fulfil'd,* viz.

Not But the Man has Malice, wou'd he
(ſhow it ;
But on my Conſcience, he's a baſhful
(Poet :
You think that ſtrange,— no matter—
(he'll out-grow it.

Prologue to the Old Batch.

ANIMAD-

ANIMADVERSIONS

O N

Mr. Congreve's

L A T E

ANSWER

T O

Mr. COLLIER, &c.

Mr. *Johnson.* COme, Mr. *Smith,* sit down ------
bring a Flask Boy, let Wit
and Wine flow together; here's
Congreve, Congreve; here's the
Man o'th' World, *the Wittol of* Old Batch.
Wittol-Hall, Gads daggers, Belts!
  B   *Blades!*

and *Scabbards! come and Embrace
my Bully, my Back, this Pen of
his I'll maintain to be the best
Divine, Anatomist, Lawyer, or Ca-
suist in* Europe; *it shall decide a
Controversie or split a Cause*——

Smith. *Nay, now I must speak,
it will split a Hair, by the Lord*
Harry, *I have seen it.*

Johns. *Oh, now I kiss your Hilts
Sir, you are floating upon the full
blown Bladders of Repentance, to
swim once more into his Favour.
O Gad! I have a great passion for*
Congreve, *don't you admire him?
Ah! he's so fine, so extreamly Fine,
so every thing in the World that
I like.*

Smith. Cowley *I believe you
mean.*

Johnson. No, no ; *our English*
Horace *I mean :* Cowley *was a very
pretty Fellow, but let me tell you,*
Com-

Comparisons are odious ; Cowley *was a very pretty Fellow in those days it must be granted ; but alas, Sir, were he now Alive, he'd be nothing, nothing in the Earth.*

Smith. *How Sir! I make a doubt if there be so great a Poet breathing.*

Johnson. O Lard! *Will Con-greve's* alive Man, he's my Coun-tryman, he has been regenerated ever since he turn'd Poet, and his *Muse* has had a new *Birth* too since the Peace.

Smith. What Miracle has made him a *Staffordshire Man,* I know not, but I'm sure his *Muse,* for all his fine Flights, is but a *Bog-trotter still.*

Johns. Fie, Fie, I don't like that (*still*) 'tis no good word, *vide* Congreve, pag. 47

B 2 *But*

But why fo fevere upon your Friend, the Courteous the obliging Mr. *Congreve?* *the very Pink of Courtefie;* nay, *the very reflection of Heaven in a Pond.*——

Johnf. Ay, ay, but he that leaps at him, is loft.

Smith. No, you miftake him, he's all *Love for Love,* not on jot of the *Double Dealer;* come, come, *edifie, and chew the cud of Underftanding;* here's *Paper Diet that will make you Fat,* here's *Congreve* againft *Collier* Man, you fhall fee how he mauls him, Egad, he does not yield the Parfon a Tythe of his Citations, *For why fhould a Blockhead have one in Ten?* You know the Song, Friend. Here, hand *Willy with the Wifp* hither to me; fo—— arm'd with this Book and this Flask, I ftand like *Jove,* with my Thunder and Light-

Lightning: Ha, Boy, here's *Bacchus* and *Apollo Virorum* for you; come, Pledge me: By the Muses, tho' this Helicon of Wit will pleaſe you better than that of Wine, come, bleſs your ſelf, and I'll open the Book.

Smith. Conjure up Parſon *Saygrace*, to crave a Bleſſing, no doubt, Mr. *Collier* will give Thanks after Meat.

Johnſ. Stay, cut open theſe two Leaves, *and I'll tell you*, (O pox! this will diſcover, (Damn the Bookſeller) my partiality in commending before I read it) *very well*——— *ſo, thank you, my Dear,* ——— *but as I was telling you*——— *piſh, this is the untoward'ſt Leaf* ——— *ſo, as I was telling you*——— *how d'ye like it now?*
Hideous———*ha, frightful ſtill, or how?*

Smith.

Smith. O no, Sir, *'tis very well as can be.*

Johnf. *And fc*—— *bnt where did I leave off, my Dear, I was telling you*——

Smith. *You were about to tell me fomething, but you left off before you began;* I am afraid your Friend Mr. *Congreve* does fo too ; come, we'll fee in the Title Page here what 'tis he drives at; *Amendments of the Citations from the Old Batchelor, Double-Dealer, Love for Love, Mourning Bride.*—— *By the Author of thofe Plays.* Who alone in the name of Wonder, can this be? Did you not tell me this was Mr. *Congreve's* Book ? I hope you will not make me believe thefe four Plays were Mr. *Congreve's.*

Johnf. Whofe are they then? *Cujus pecus?*

Will.

Smith. *Non Melebæi*———·You know what *Hartwell* ſays, this Brat's *mighty like his Grace, has juſt his Smile and Air of's Face, has ſuch a one's Noſe and Eyes, and Mr. What de call's Mouth to a tittle.* In ſhort, thoſe Plays *are little Compounds of the whole Body of Scriblers :* Nay, even *Tom. Du——y* has not been proof againſt his Stealths, and I would have him reflect Mr. *Congreve's* Motto upon him, *viz.*

Thoſe pretty things Friend Congreve
   you rehearſe,
*W*ere once *my* Words, tho' *they are*
   now your Verſe.

Well, now to page 1. here he ſays, *Some would think him idle if he labour'd for an Anſwer to Mr.* Collier ; intimating, that Mr. *Col-*

lier would upon his own Evidence be Condemn'd, and he Acquitted before he could make his Defence,—— and pray why so? all the World are not *Staffordshire* Men, and 'twill be no easie Task to make them so

But to agree with him, if he were acquitted at all, it must have been before he offered at his Defence; for he has made so mean and wretched a businefs of it, that he is now Cast in the Opinion of the World: He has said nothing that can hinder Sentence from being past upon him, even in the Opinion of his bigotted Friends.

Johnf. Well, but perufe him from page 2. to 7.

Smith. Yes, I fee he very dully Afperfes Mr. *Collier* all the way; and at the end, to clofe the *Cli-*

max

max of the Abuſe, he calls him Mr. *Collier.* Now 'tis my Opinion, that Mr. *Collier* knows himſelf very well, and needs not that Advice which may juſtly be given to Mr. *Congreve.*

Ne te quæſiveris extra.

For indeed he is *Tantum mutatus ab illo,* that he ſeems to be no more his Father's Offspring, than the Plays he owns are his.

Before I proceed, for Method ſake, I muſt premiſe ſome few things, which if you think in your Conſcience too much to be granted me, I deſire you to proceed no further, but you may return to Mr. Congreve's Book a lone, &c.　v.Cong: P.7.

Johnſ.

Johnſ. Well, go on, you'll come to *Greek* preſently, 'tis very Witty I believe, but I can't read it,——

Smith. κατὰ πᾶσαν κακίαν I wonder Mr. *Congreve* has not inſtructed his Friends in the meaning of that; why, it relates to all kinds of Vice; O yes, here 'tis Conſtru'd, look here Mr. *Johnſon.*

Johnſ. Well what think you now of his four *Poſtulata's?*

Smith. Why, he plays a ſure Card, he's at all-Fours with Mr. *Collier* I think, Higheſt, Loweſt——

Johnſ. Jack and the Game boy, ——ay, ay, he ſteers a right courſe, he can give him a Broad-ſide, let the Winds blow how they will.

Smith. Ay, right, but *he ſends his Wits for a Venture,* and I fear they will be plaguily Weather-beaten before they come home; here

here he is run a-ground already, I see, and beats upon the Sands, and for fear of being made Prize, has set out false Colours, *viz.* His third *Postulatum,* where he desires Mr. *Collier's* Citations may be absolutely thought false, that is, may appear in Mr. *Congreve's* own Colours: Now his Answering Mr. *Collier,* must certainly be ridiculously vain, if this is granted; for any Man, to clear the Aspersion of being Scabby, need only expose his Hands, and turn up his Back-side, to prove his Cleanness. But he's Affronted I suppose to be turn'd up by Mr. *Collier,* because taking him unawares, the dirty Linnen appears in view.

Johns. Hold, hold, good Friend, you lash too hard; *our Jehu too will turn Hackney-Coachman* I fear.

If

If my Friend has been in fault, and is taken up to be Whip'd, and has nothing elſe to ſay ; he piouſly crys out, *Jeſu*, and like other good Natur'd Boys, pro-miſes never to do't again.

Smith. But if he has ſtill the itch to ſteal and publiſh on, and ſcan other Men's Proſe on his own Unpoetical Fingers, he does it ſo roughly, they muſt needs break out to Soreneſs.

Et vivos roderet ungues, &c.

For Example, I'll repeat you one or two of his ſmooth Lines.

Old Batch. P. 8.

For Love's Iſland : I for the Gol-den Coaſt.

Now,

Now if you can get a Shore on that Island without being plaguily out of Breath, I'll be bound to find out the Golden Coast for Mr. *Congreve.*

Let's have a fair Trial, and a clear (Sea. Prol. to Double Dealer.

There's a Line for you, that has sayl'd it self into a clear Sea of Prose.

Johnf. No indeed, 'tis a Verse, I'm sure, for it Rhymes to three lines going before.

Smith. O then the Rhyme does the businefs, or elfe *I'gad let me tell you Mr.* Congreve's *flanding Argument is depref's'd in dumb fhew:* If this Claim won't pafs in the Court of *Parnaffus,* I'm afraid we fhall fee him expell'd the Land at the next Vifitation of *Apollo.*

Johnf.

Johns. Come read on, 'tis mighty fine I think, and as my dear Friend *Setter* says, *my Head runs on nothing else, nor can I talk of nothing else.*

Old Batc. P. 47.

Smith. That (*Nor*) makes it excellent English—— *nor Du——y nor M——ux* themselves, *nor* the insufferable Dullness of *P——x*, *nor* the Lightness both in Head and Tail of the presuming *T----r*, could have brought in *Nor* more elegantly.

Well, as to his fourth *Postulatum*, we'll see what he says there, I'll pass his two first, for he may have half-way given him in his Race, and be easily run down too. To shew himself a Man of Letters, he talks of the Alphabet here in the fourth place, and says, that tho' he claps a Scripture Sentence into the Mouths of of Persons in a Play (which, by the by, may be Bawds or Whores) 'tis allowable, becaufe the fame Letters are requifite to the fpelling of all Words whatever. Here Mr. *Congreve* feems not to underftand his *A. B. C.* for tho' the Bread and Wine may be received in the Church before the Altar, yet 'tis not to be offered in a Play-Houfe, or any other place of Sport, much lefs be fwallow'd by fuch whofe touch would Pollute it; for once Confecrated, it immediately ceafes to be common.

Johnf. Nay, if you won't allow him his Heads, the Body of his Difcourfe is ruin'd.

Smith. His Heads? why I can find neither Head nor Tail in't for my part, 'tis a beaftly fort of a Monfter that crawls on all *Four*; and

and only licks the Duft, which it felf raifes.

In his 13th. page, he fays, he has written but four poor Plays, here indeed the Man were modeft, had he not faid *Written*. Well, four Plays; in how many Years? About eight; does he not hammer out his *Minerva's*?

Johnf. Why; 'tis neceffary a good Play fhould be a twelve Month or two a Writing; but go on with the Book, come turn over a new Leaf and don't rail.

Smith. Well; in the next page Mr. *Collier*, he fays, is in the right, and he agrees with him, and immediately after he fays he does not underftand him, and can make no anfwer to him.

He Juggles finely it feems, fometimes there is fomething in
his

his Cups, and then whip it's gone again. The Gentleman under-ftands *Legerdemain* fure.

Johnf. I know not what you'd be at. Sir, with your Jugling, and your Cups, pray, what do you mean?

Smith. Why, I believe your Friend *Will* was in his Cups when he wrote this. *P.* 15. He makes a great fplutter about big Whores, and becaufe there are three of them that are of the big-geft, and but four in all, he would put them upon Mr. *Collier*; nay, fure they'll be reconcil'd foon; now he parts with his Whores; but hold, I fee 'tis out of a fly de-fign, he has made them Whores, and now would put them on him; a cunning Shaver, and knows how to difpofe of a Wench when he's tir'd of her: Here he runs on

C   like

like an Arithmetician, builds upon a falſe Multiplication Table of Three of the biggeſt of Four, runs to Diviſions and Subſtractions, and caſts up Accounts, which he places to Mr. *Collier*, and which really when Examined, turn only to a Cypher.

Here he changes his Tune again, and after he has blown the VVorld up with falſe Muſick, he lets his Pipe fall, and ſays, *He loves to meddle with his Match.* He ſays, *It was a Mercy all the four VVomen were not Nought.* It was ſo indeed, ſince Mr. *Congreve* had any Buſineſs with them. Towards the end of the Paragraph, he muſters up *Furies* and *Harpies*; and after he has ſhewn his little Reading, he brings in honeſt *Ariſtotle*, with his *ipſe dixit*, to paſs a Compliment on VVomen, and ſay, there

are

are more bad than good in the
VVorld : This very piece of Breeding is what he taxes Mr. *Collier*
with juſt before. But his Opinion perhaps may be as his Song
goes,

The Nymph may be Chaſte that has Love for
never been Try'd. Love.

Which Senſe, *Ovid* writing after
Mr. *Congreve*, had occaſion to
borrow, but to hide his Theft,
he made Latin of it, and put
it in an Elegy. *Caſta eſt quam
nemo rogavit.* Book 1ſt. Elegy 8.
And becauſe he ſeems to value
himſelf for the niceneſs of his
Breeding, I'll quote you a place
out of the *Old Batchelor,* ſhall
give you a ſtrong proof of his
good Manners; *Hartwell* ſays,

C 2   *My*

Old Batch..
P. 7. *My Talent is chiefly that of
speaking Truth, which I don't ex-
pect shou'd ever recommend me to
People of Quality———— I thank
Heaven, I have very honestly pur-
chased the Hatred of all the
Great Families in Town.*

The Gentleman is extreamly
well bred, and the Lord C----
to whom it was Dedicated, had,
no doubt, an extraordinary Compliment of it. But here, in the
18th page, he begins to look a-
bout him and refer to his first
Proposition with a Witness.

Johns. How do you mean with
a Witness? What because he
quotes *Moliere?*

Smith. Ay, as the Proverb
goes, *Ask my Brother if I am a
Thief.* But prithee, dost think
thy

thy Friend *Will* has no other mark of the *French*, but a small Citation?

Johnf. None that he is willing to produce Sir; go on prithee, here you shall see he's a Sophister; in short, he's every thing; see here how he argues about a *Pimp* and *a Poet*, and when he has talk'd towards the end, a little, of *Worshiping the Devil*, he conculdes——

Smith. Like the Grave-digger in *Hamlet*, very Gravely with an *Ergol*, &c. Truly I think, that Grave-digger and he, were the fitteft Persons to caft up their Dirt and their Arguments together. In his pretty concife Sentence of three Lines, immediately following, he Snaps and Snarls like an angry Cur, that will fuffer none to pafs

Page, 20.

C 3   in

in quiet but his own Mungrel
Breed. But, tis not Mr. *Collier*,
as he would have it, but he
himself that ought to be *Lick'd*,
Vide Ans.
p. 21. but not with an *Absolution*.

Answ.
p. 23. *O Law! here's the poor* Mourning Bride *tax'd with Smut and
Prophaneness, Alack! and a Well-
a-day! Nay, if there be Immodesty
in my Tragedy too, I shall never
write any thing Modestly while
I have a Being. Poor* Will *what
do the Damn'd endure, but to Despair.*

In Page 26. he's got to his
Letters again: Who knows but
he may be able to write something with Modesty and De-
cency as he calls it? If he can
but get back again the Skill
that he wittily gives to Mr. *Collier,*

lier, in *Anagram*, there may be
some hopes still. Here he seems
more than ordinary mov'd: That
his Poetry should be Criticiz'd
upon, is ten times worse than the
Prophaneness, but *the corruption
of an incorrigible Plagiary is the Ge-
neration of a Sowr Poet.*

Here he seems to take a breathing a little, and for refreshment
sake, I suppose, *wafts the Air* to
and fro with a couple of *Epithets,*
till he cools himself into a consent
with Mr. *Collier* in a very short
time; and indeed he has need on't,
for he seems to be in a very fiery
Passion: But I find, *Non potest &
forbere & flare.* He might have
kept his breath to have cool'd his
Potage.

Here in the self same Paragraph
he breaks the new made League,
and that very affair which just

now he confented to, he fays, at the clofe to Mr. *Collier's* Charge as Nonfenfe. Prithee don't tell your Friend *Congreve* I find fault with his Book, for if it be his *Irifh-Staffordfhire* way of boxing, to fhake hands firft, and hit one a flap in the Face, I'll be fure to keep out of his Clutches. He's *a dainty Critick indeed?* 'Tis with him and his *Mufe*, as he fays,——

O let us not fupport, but fink each other lower yet, down, down, where levell'd low, &c.

Prethee, what would his *Mufe* and he have? Are they not low enough already? I am fure if her wings were cut, as Mr. *Collier* has juftly mark'd them, we fhould have fewer of his flights to Heaven or Hell, till he were better convinc'd whe-

ther

ther the Torture of the *Damn'd* were, *but knowing Heaven, to know it loft for ever.*

Here he falls a *Jefting, and letting off Puns and Crackers,* he has got *a Whip and a Bell too,* and indeed I think they are in very good hands. Since he by his own confeffion, *and in his own dog Language,* can *teach a Spaniel to fet.* So, he's got into his Element again. What will he fay to this here, where he would make two of Mr. *Collier ?* I don't find that he has hack'd, and hew'd him fo, that he's like to fall one jot a-pieces; rather, *crefcit fub pondere virtus.* Two to one they fay is odds at Foot-Ball, and I fancy Mr. *Collier* unmultiply'd has given him tof-fes enough to make him fhun him, but poor *Will.* when the Ball

Ball is lost, will venture to kick
at his Shins, for I don't under-
derstand how he can make Mr.
Collier the Divine any other Man
than what he is, so as to af-
sume another Person to turn
Critick in, and yet remain Mr.
Collier the Divine, all the while;
if he can spin this double spi-
der's Web out of the Bowels of
his Invention, I should allow
that he had some guts in his
Brains, and consent with him,
where he says, p. 51. *Nature has
been provident only to Bears and
Spiders.* Here's a rare boy for
you again.

Anfw.
p. 31.

*Epithets make Prose languish-
ing, and cold; and the frequent
use of them in Prose, makes it
pretend too much, and approach too
near to Poetry,* Sure the Gentleman forgot himself here, the
Ague

Ague of inervate coldnefs, not
the Feaver of Paffion has feiz'd
him now, but he has been knea-
ding up his Profe fo long, that
in fpite of all his fhaking, it
will ftick upon his hands ; for
that the fame thing *fhould make
Profe languifhing and cold, and
yet approach too near to any Poetry,* (but Mr. *Congreve's*) is as
ftrange to me, as that the fame
acquaintance between Mr. *Charles
Hopkins* and him, fhould make
the former, through too much
good Nature, and willingnefs to
raife his *Friend* as he *thought
him,* Dedicate, and Afcribe to
him, what he really owes to
Nature only ; and the *latter* very impudently, in publick ; to
fay he was very angry with him
for the prefumption. A very
pretty Fellow truly this. Now,

I

been forc'd to own the same thing.

Johns. Prethee mind the Book, and read that, not the Man, don't make him worse than he is, or you'll run into as bad a diftinction as you fay he does, when he divides Mr. *Collier* the Divine, and Mr. *Collier* the Critick, for here you make a difference between the *Poet*, and Mr. *Congreve.*

Smith. O there's a great deal of difference, but perhaps I don't pretend to make them the *same person.* Befides, he takes Mr. *Collier's* perfon to task, and why fhould not I infpect him a little, 'tis not his fnarling at the Town in a fulfom Dedication to a damn'd Play, when he fhould Addrefs to his Patron all the while, that fhall make me fpare him,

him, neither am I bound to believe him when he says in the
same Dedication—— *If I really
wish it might have had a more
popular reception ; it is not at all
in consideration of my self ; but* Dedica.
because I wish well, and would Double
gladly contribute to the benefit of Dealer.
*the Stage, and diversion of the
Town.* There's your *Double Dealer* for you, never was Poets
Character better drawn by himself, *since the Ignorance and Malice
of the greater part of the Audience* Ibid.
*grew such, that they would make
a Man turn Herald to his own
Play, and blazon every Character.*
I'll no more believe his late De-
claration to the World and his
Patron, than I believ'd him,
when he said he'd go as far as
New-Market to see a Play which
a Friend of mine writ ; but perhaps

haps Mr. *Congreve* thought himself particularly concern'd, which
made him mention *New-Market*,
when the Horse-Races were run
there, this Gentleman, he said,
(as he had heard) declar'd to *set
up in opposition to him* in the o-
ther House, so, 'tis likely, Mr.
Congreve thought his Poetry in
danger: But, *set up, what?* Not
himself, in opposition to Mr. *Congreve.* I dare excuse my Friend
from that Grand Presumption,
or the open profession of it at
least; he only, as being a Poet,
design'd indeed to set up his *Pegasus* at the other House, pray,
what was that to Mr. *Congreve*:
O, but when he talk'd of opposition to his House, perhaps
'twas something to the Beast he
rides on. Now in my opinion,
it would be well if he could bridle
his

his Tongue, and not spur himself, as well as his *Rosinante*, out
of breath; nor would I have
him think others, (who may have
better Coursers) must be rid out
o'the stirrups, because he has
got so much the start of them;
and I know not how it might
have gone, if my Friend had given him the Challenge, (tho' he
never design'd more than an
ayring) but I dare swear he
would have sweated least, and
yet I'll allow too what *Hartwell*
says,

(*run,*)
All Coursers the first heat with vigour
But 'tis with Whip and Spur the Race
(*is won.*)

the Gentleman too thought Mr.
Congreve not his Enemy at least,
because when he was first re-
D   com-

commended to him by a Friends
Letter, the mighty Man of Wit
was pleas'd to say he'd give him
what affiftance poffibly he could
in his Art, (as he was pleas'd
to call it) when in the end, at
the Reprefentation of this Play
of my Friend's, he was feen
very gravely with his Hat over
his Eyes among his chief Actors,
and Actreffes, together with the
two She Things, call'd *Poeteffes*,
which Write for his Houfe,
as 'tis nobly call'd ; thus feated
in State among thofe and fome
other of his Ingenious critical
Friends, they fell all together
upon a full cry of Damnation,
but when they found the malicious Hifs would not take, this
very generous, obliging Mr. *Con-*
greve was heard to fay, *We'll*
find out a New way for this Spark,
                              take

take my word there is a way of clapping of a Play down.——This was heard by very creditable Perfons, but his Malice could no way prevail, for fpite of him, and all other difadvantages the Play furviv'd with Applaufe, and overcame his Envy.

But to go on with his Book, here he talks of *puffing and blowing, and laying about in fhort Sentences,* fure he has been an Apprentice to a Blackfmith that he's always ftirring the Coals thus, only to make himfelf more fmutty; but the mifchief on't is, he can never ftrike the Iron while 'tis hot: Well, I begin to be tyr'd of him, and fhall only run him flightly over, *and take notice of his errors, where they fhall appear blazing* in his polite Pages.

Johnf.

Anf. Pag. 28.

Johnf. *You are undoubtedly in the right to take juft as much as ferves your own turn.* But I don't hear you commend at all.

Smith. No truly, I can't commend a dull thing, if I know it to be fuch; I can't forbear falling a-fleep over the *Double Dealer*, tho' *Dryden* has writ a fine Commendatory Copy before it: Where the paint's lay'd on fo very thick, 'tis a fign the Face is a very fcurvy one; and as for *Dryden*, why he'd give *Du——y* a Copy of Verfes if he would cringe to him, pray did he not write one to'ther day, prefix'd to as wretched a piece of Stuff of a Play, as ever a *Tennis-Court Theatre* toft into the World?

Here in page 38. he mufters up a Speech *of the crying Sin of Adultery.* Shows us that Mr. *Collier*

lier has left a rank broken and imperfect, and refers us to the Play, as the main body to make the breach up from thence. A pretty fort of an Anfwer this; Is Mr. *Congreve* fo affur'd that every Body has his foolifh Plays by them? Or does he think thofe that have, will take the pains? Pray, whofe Bufin.fs is it? 'tis they that Anfwer Mr. *Collier*, if they do, not he——— Ah! poor Man! *Indeed I cannot forbear Laughing when I compare his dreadful Comment with fuch poor filly words as are in the Text.*— But hold, what's here? is our *Democritus* turn'd *Heraclytus* already? Alas! Anf. Pag. 39.

Let fable Clouds her chalky Cliffs adorn. Paftora.

D 3   Which

Which with his foregoing Line, which makes up the burthen of the Song, is Stol'n from a Poem written on the Death of *General Monk*; but I need not detect him in Particulars, what has he publish'd that is not Stol'n? Alas! this is so Melancholy, 'tis almost next to *Dead*, *Dead*, *Dead*. Well, if I can constrain my Tears, I'll read it you *in totidem Verbis.*

Ibid.   *——Especially when I reflect how young a beginner, and how very much A Boy I was when that Comedy was Written, which several know, was some Years before it was Acted: When I wrote it, I had little thoughts of the Stage; but did it to amuse my self in a slow recovery from a fit of Sickness. Afterwards*

terwards through my Indiscretion,
it was seen; and in some little
time more, it was Acted. And
I through the remainder of my Indiscretion, suffer'd my self to be
drawn in, to the prosecution of a
difficult and thankless Study.

Poor *Billy*! why I protest,
the poor Boy has been hardly
dealt with. I'm afraid it has
met with a Step-mother Muse;
But what would it be at? would
it have its Backside stuck with
Points? Or would it have the
Ladies o'th' Town send it Bread
and Butter with Glass Windows
wrought on't? Or what other
Gugaw would it have? Mr.
Collier has given it a Coral to
make it cut its Teeth kindly,
and a Rattle to quiet it, but
these it is not pleas'd with.

Well,

Anf. Pag. 40.
Well, here's another piece of Mr. *Congreve's* Kindnefs, he's very glad Mr. *Collier* has fome devotion for the Lips and Eyes of a pretty Woman ; the Wag talks fo pleafingly of it, that he licks his own Lips at her till he makes his Teeth water, and yet he gives her up to Mr. *Collier* ; what won't he do to be Reconcil'd ?

Well, *with reverence to your Friend the Author be it fpoken* ; Ibid. Immediately following here, he confeffes himfelf to have writ ftark Nonfenfe. I wonder now what's become of all his wonted Fury, he has not been very angry for a pretty while, but as he fays, perhaps *Paffion comes upon him by Infpiration.* I wonder if Dulnefs does not fo too.

Here

Here he repeats a Citation out of the *Old Batchelor*, and says,

There are some things promis'd in some body's Name.

Now, to excuse himself from the abuse of the *Catechism*, he wisely says only—— *I meant* *Ans. Pag.* *no ill in this Allegory, nor do I* [42.] *perceive any in it now.* To return his own ill Expression on him which he uses on this occasion, he has prov'd but a very bad *Godfather*, to promise some thing, and perform nothing, but poorly excuse himself with pleading Ignorance, when he should rather correct the Brats he has promis'd for, than wilfully (meerly to be rid of them) have

have them confirm'd in their
unbounded Wickedness. So,—
here's another Paragraph I'll read
you *verbatim*.

*Anſ. Pag.
42.*   *In the* Double Dealer, *Mr.*
Collier ſays, *Lady* Plyant *crys
out* Jeſu, *and talks Smut in the
ſame Sentence. That Exclamation I give him up freely. I had
my ſelf long ſince condemn'd it,
and reſolv'd to ſtrike it out in
the next Impreſſion. I will not
urge the Folly, Viciouſneſs or Af-
fectation of the Character to ex-
cuſe it. Here I think my ſelf
oblig'd to make my Acknowledg-
ments for a Letter which I receiv'd after the publication of
this Play, relating to this very
Paſſage. It came from an Old
Gentlewoman and a Widow, as*
ſhe

*she said, and very well to pass:
It contain'd very good Advice, and
requir'd an Answer, but the Di-
rection for the Superscription was
forgot. If the good Gentlewoman
is yet in being, I desire her to
receive my Thanks for her good
Council, and for her approbation
of all the Comedy, that word
alone excepted.*

This is a pretty tale of a
Tub, is it not? In the first
place, the word *Jesu* is no less
than thrice Prophanely mention'd in this Comedy, which
I never heard that any body
but *Dryden* and this good old
Woman ever yet approv'd of.
Well, 'twere something could
we hope this word, which he
applies so ill, would be dash'd

out

out of the next Impreffion;
but hold, I forget my felf,
who will ever be at the charge
of another Impreffion of fuch
a piece of heavy Stuff as the
Double Dealer ? Well,—— here's
a moft furprizing Turn, here's
an old Woman (becaufe, as
fhe faid, very well to pafs)
courted at a moft extravagant
rate : But poor *Will* was very
hard put to it here, that he
might not make his Con-
feffion, and owe his Thanks
to Mr. *Collier* ; and being thus
heavily puzzl'd, and in the dark,
thought *Joan* was as good
there as my Lady. After he
had been a good while, as I
imagin, between Hawk and
Buzard, he e'en wifely turn'd
to the to the latter. But what

a

a wretched condition muſt he
certainly have been in, when
he was forc'd to frame ſo idle
a Story, chiefly for the ſake of
a pretence to make us believe
in the tail of the Paragraph,
that he had an Old Womans
approbation of all the Comedy,
that word alone excepted? I
think he had better have yielded thankfully to Mr. *Collier,*
but he's of his own Mr. *Brisk's*
temper, where he ſays,

Egad, I love to be Malicious, Double
——*nay, the Deuce take me, there's* Dealer,
Wit in't too—— *and Wit muſt be* Pag. 8.
foil'd by Wit; cut a Diamond
with a Diamond: No other way
Egad.——

Egad,

Egad; there's a Diamond for
you now, pray what Diamond
can cut that? I'm afraid the
World Exclaims, (or I'm sure
they have reason) at the un-
equal'd Prophaneness of his Ex-
pressions, worse than the *Lady
Plyant* does in his Play, *viz.*

Double
Dealer.
Page, 21. *But I have not Patience——
Oh! the Impiety of it! as I was
saying, and the unparallel'd Wickedness! Then follows, O Mer-
ciful Father!*

A very pretty Exclamation,
that——when the Person speaking, Dissembled all the while,
and taxes another with what
she knew to be false. I shall
only desire your Friend to
consider, what the same Lady
says a little after.

O

O reflect upon the horror of that and then the guilt of deceiving every Body.

Here he seems to be at Questions and Commands, a playing with Mr. *Collier* , and because the latter has not given a pawn for my Lady *Plyant's* loose talk, your Friend *Will* pretends to *Smut* him, 'tis a very dirty trick of him, that you will own at least. *Anf. Pag. 43.*

Well, here he pretends to excuse the Character of a Fool in his Play, (saying upon all, and upon no occasions, —— *I am beholding to Providence , truly , I am mightily beholding to Providence.*) *Ibid.*

dence.) only by, catching at a flip which perhaps the Printer might have been guilty of, not Mr. *Collier*, the meaning is plain however, but fuch a Foe as your Friend *Will* once driven to difpair, will give no quarter, but catch at all advantages. Well, if this Prophanenefs of his, ben't reputed to him as Sin, (without Repentance,) he will have reafon in earneft to take the words of his Fool into his own Mouth, and fay, *truly I am mightily beholding to Providence.*

But here the afpiring Hotheaded driver runs on in his Career, more mad than *Phaethon*, lafhing the Scripture with Burlefque, calling *Jehu a Hackney*

ney-Coachman, he really does what the other Mad-man was only feign'd to have done, he drives at Heaven to confound it with the wildneſs of his Courſe; and might he be ſuffer'd to go on, he would ſet the World on Fire; but as the ſaying is, I hope, there will be a ſpoke put in his Wheel. Mr. *Collier* has Thunder'd him pretty well, but like the other raſh miſtaken Boy, he runs headlong on, becauſe forſooth he thinks himſelf a *Brat of Apollo's*. Well then, becauſe we ſuppoſe our ſelf to have ſprung from this radiant God, we may be preſumptuous, and *Paſſion may come upon us by Inſpiration.*

E   Well;

Well, see this same High-born
Babe, with not one of his Father's Rays about him, or any
thing elfe of the God, but the
fiery Rage, when he's at a
lofs how to Guide.

Anf. Pag.
45. *Infpiration fignifies no more
than Breathing into*; Now, if
if it be fo, I believe when
Mr. *Congreve* was *Infpir'd* with
Poetry, he was only *Breath'd
into*; but whether it might be
the back way or no, I leave
to the Opinion of the World.
He has got a Dog-trick of
turning round fometimes before he lyes down, as refer-
ring, (when all his other *Breathing into* is gone) to fome of
his fine Propofitions.

Well,

Well, after his reference
to his *Postulatum*, sure you
would think he were lay'd;
Ay, but he gets up again to
Bark a little; he renews the
Discourse, meerly to shew
his knowledge of a *Puppet-
show*, where he owns he can
only argue as the *Puppet* did
with the *Rabbi*; *It is Prophane,* *Ans. Page*
and it is not Prophane. This is *pro* ⁴⁶·
and *con*, that's the Truth on't,
but if he would do as Mr.
Brisk desires, that is, give us
Marginal Notes; it might be
some Satisfaction.

So, to excuse himself here
from Mr. *Collier*, in his saying,

Tho' Marriage makes Man and
Wife one Flesh, it leaves them
still two Fools.

He

He is forc'd to detect his Theft, and confeſs that he Borrow'd it from *Ben Johnſon*, who ſays in one of his Plays, *Man and Wife make one Fool.*

Anſ. Page 48. Well, here *Scandal* ſays, he'll *die a Martyr rather than diſclaim his Paſſion.* Now, what Martyr the *Greek* word may ſignifie, I muſt beg leave to contradict Mr. *Congreve*, and ſay, that in plain *Engliſh, that is,* plain cuſtomary Acceptation, it does not ſignifie Witneſs, but Martyr, *that is,* as our common Notion of the word bears, one who dies for his Religion. But Mr. *Congreve* is ſo angry, and ſo near Swearing about it, that he will needs have it for a Witneſs; well,

well, he's a fiery Gentleman, *and would rather die a Martyr than difclaim his Paffion.*

Here again he's put to't to confefs where he borrow'd the word *Whorefon*; from *Shakefpear* and *Johnfon*. Well, but he has us'd it fo lately, that I fhan't difpute his Title to't by any means.

Hey day! what have we got here? *Jeremy Congreve*, who's that prithee, doft know?

Johnf. No, faith, my Friend's Name is *Will.*

Smith. No, no, 'tis *Jeremy*, 'tis certainly *Jeremy*, I'll call him fo, becaufe there's Wit in't; Oh, 'tis very Ingenious when I would rally a Man, to fay, *He can't call me* Jeremy Congreve; *let him call me* Anf. Page 50.

E 3   *what*

what he will, he can't call me
Jeremy Congreve.

I find he rallies more like a
Waterman than a Gentleman, and
and argues more like a Pedant
than a Scholar.

Here again, he defires the
Reader to look over his Plays,
to find Citations; fet the Im-
pudence on't afide, 'tis a very pretty way of Evafion;
when he's caught in the Net,
if poffible, he gives a flounce
out, and the Standers by, if
they pleafe, may go feek for
him in his *own Mud*; but as
the faying is, I fancy moft
have other Fifh to fry.

Here

Here he talks of a Speech of Sir *Sampson's* ; in the Play 'tis said,

The Sampsons *were strong Dogs from the Beginning.*

And so on with more such Prophane Stuff ; but let Mr. *Congreve* take notice how Sir *Sampson* is Answer'd, for 'tis *well if he does not pull an old House over his Head.*

Here he's a Star-gazing with as much care as Sir *Sydrophel's* *Watchum* himself, to know whether *Solomon* had his Wisdom by *Astrology* or no ; or perhaps it may be to find out whether or not he was Wise ; for, to banter the Scripture, and ridicule the Knowledge of

Ans. Pag. 52.

E 4   So-

Solomon ; I remember where he says,

All that he knew was, that he knew nothing.

and that Stol'n too from the laft Lines of the *Emperor of the Moon.*

I wifh Mr. *Congreve* knew as much of himfelf, I am fure it were not amifs to tell him fo ; for in fpight of all his *Aftrology*, I fear in the end he may come to Curfe his Stars.

Well, here Valentine fays *I am Truth.* This is in all Mens Opinion, whom I have hear'd fpeak of it, horrid Prophanity, and I think fcarce any Body but a *Wittol* would have put

such

such words in a Madman's
Mouth: Poorly to excuse it,
he says he had first written,
I am Tom-tell-troth. I dare pre- Ans. Pag. 56.
sume, Mr. *Congreve* is not *Truth,*
when he says so, nor will I
allow him the Title (which he
himself as he owns has blot-
ted out) of *Tom-tel-troth* neither. As Mr. *Congreve* allows
Inspiration to be but *Breathing
into,* certainly I believe, when
he was *Inspir'd* to write this,
he was *breath'd into by the Devil.*

A pretty Humour this next
of his, *viz.*

In the next Chapter he quotes Ans. Page 57.
me so little, and has so little
reason even for that little, that
'tis hardly worth Examining.

This

This is all very *little* I must confess, but while Mr. *Congreve* seems to slight it, and give no Answer, he is rais'd so upon that *little*, that he looks very *big* upon't. I find he grows a *little* weary of his Adversary tho', for he is not rather for playing at small Game than stand out.

Johns. Sure you'll be pleas'd at last, come prithee read it out.

Smith. Pleas'd! no Faith, but I'm almost a-sleep, prithee drink to me, all this stuff is so plaguy dry and insipid, I want something to put my mouth in Taste.

Here's a long business all the way from pag. 60, to pag. 78. Whether or not Parsons should be be Expos'd upon the Stage; I shall leave that to Mr. *Collier* (in the Answer I am told he designs) to determine ; I shall only give my private Opinion that they should not ; for, to bring a Minister to ridicule him upon the Stage, must be meerly the effect of the Author's Contempt of the Clergy, and desire that the Audience should despise them them too, for what we have in Derision we Contemn : there is certainly no necessity for making the Priest or the Chaplain appear on the Stage ; for, the Ceremony for which they're generally hook'd in, (that's Marriage) is never perform'd in the presence of the Audience ; and as to Exposing their Faults,

me, tho' some of the Town
be your Friend *Will*'s Bigots,
yet they will not continue so,
when

Ans. Page
83.
He shall appear mounted upon
a false Pegasus, *like a* Lanca-
shire *Witch upon an imaginary*
Horse, the Fantom shall be Un-
bridled, and the Broomstick made
visible.

Well, he continues his fine
Division of Mr. *Collier* for some
Pages ; I wonder what he
makes of him at last, he'll
rise in his Arithmetick to his
own Golden Rule by and by
perhaps, and make him in the
first ten Lines, the chief of the
Gyants that fought against the
Gods, and in the following.
Ten

Ten, the *Mars* that overthrew the *Gyants* ; this he could do admirably well in a *Poem on Namur*, and why not here ?

Johnf. And yet you fay he fteals every thing, now I dare fwear he did not fteal that ?

Smith. Yes, doubtlefs, he ftole both the chief *Gyant* and *Mars*, but for his own particular fancy he thought fit to make but One of thofe Two, juft as he thought fit here to make Two of Mr. *Collier* : By this, I am afraid, that Mr. *Collier* appear'd more dreadful to him, than both *Mars* and the *Gyant* together.

But, *pitiful and mean comparifons*, (viz. *Mars* and the chief *Gyant*) *proceed from pitiful and mean*

Anf. Page 85.

*mean Ideas, and such Ideas have
their beginning from a familia-
rity with such Objects. From this
Author's poor and filthy Metaphors
and Similitudes we may learn the
filthiness of his Imagination ;
and from the uncleanness of that,
we may make a reasonable guess
at his rate of Education, and
those Objects with which he has
been most conversant and familiar.*

Anf. Page 88. Here he says a great deal of
Valentine, to vindicate him, but
I shan't trouble my self with
it, e'en let the two Madmen
go together for me, *with the
Curse of all kind tender-hearted
Women,* which he modestly calls
the *Pox,* and which he won-
ders Mr. *Collier* could write at
length, doubtless, Mr. *Collier*
would

would not rob Mr. *Congreve* of his *Pox*; for he knew it to be his, and that he deferv'd it to the full, and at length.

Here he has got a Cat to Mew out a *Spanish* Proverb for him, and I dare fwear the one underftands the Language as well as 'tother, but any thing to fhew our learning; tho' it be a Cat one while that fhall ftorm a Town, and the next *Minute Mars* and the *Gyant*. But he's of his dear *Sharpers's* opinion—— *this ex-* Old Batch. *cellent Talent of railing was born* p. 38. *with him, and he muft needs confefs he has taken care to improve it, to qualifie him for the Society of Ladies.*

F   Now

Now I think all the Citations in your Friends Book are over, and *to give him his due, he seems every where to write more from Prejudice than Opinion; he Rails when he should Reason, and for gentle reproofs, uses scurrilous reproaches. He looks upon his Adversaries to be his Enemies, and to justifie his Opinion in that particular, before he has done with them, he makes them so. If there were any Spirit in his Arguments, it would eva, porate and fly off unseen, through the heat of his Passion. His Passion does not only make him appear to be in many places in the wrong, but it also makes him appear to be conscious of it.*

That which shews the face of Wit in his writing, has indeed

no more than the Face, for the
Head is wanting ; he has put
himself to some pain to shew his
reading ; and his reading is such,
it puts us to pain to behold it.
He discovers an ill tast in Books,
and a worse Digestion. He has
swallow'd so much of the scum of
Authors, that the overflowing of
his own Gall was superfluous to make
it rise upon his Stomach.

Mr. Congreve's *vanity in pre-
tending to Criticism, has extreamly betray'd his Ignorance in the
Art of Poetry :* This is manifest
to all that understand it, and I
am not the only One who look
on this Pamphlet of his to be
a Gun level'd at the whole Clergy, while the Shot only glances
on Mr. Collier. Persecution may

make

make Men *perfevere in the* wrong; Men *may, by ill ufage be irritated fometimes to affert, and maintain even their very errors.* Perhaps *there is a vicious Pride of triumphing in the worft of the Argument, which is very prevailing with the Vanity of Mankind;* I *connot help thinking that our Author is not without his fhare of this Vanity,*——

And fo, Friend *Will*, I return you your Pamphlet.

Johnf. Well, and how do you like it in grofs, fpeak your mind.

Smith. Why, he has follow'd Capt. *Vanbrook* moft fervilely, in every thing—— but his Wit, and Gentleman-like ftile, and 'tis no matter if he had follow'd low'd the Gentleman Capt. *Vanbrook* talks of, who went Poet-Laureat to *Ruſſia* with the *Czar*. *He has very plainly ſhewn himſelf to the view of the World, and in that he has loſt himſelf*; he was unfit to play at *Blindmans-buff* with the *Muſes*, who could not fare well, but he muſt cry out Roaſtmeat.

I muſt indeed confeſs, I think, Mr. *Collier* is a little too ſevere, when he would have the Play-Houſes pull'd down. In truth, rather than remain ſo horridly wicked as they are, with ſuch Actors, and ſuch Actreſſes, I ſhould be of his Opinion: but my Sentence paſſes, as it was once given at *Rome*, of *Carthage*—— *Non delendam, ſed Carthaginem eſſe non timendam.*

F 3   The

The incomparable Author of the *Whole Duty of Man.* *Sund.* 2d *Lect.* 35. does not complain of the Theatre, as an Evil, where, if there had been reaſon, he had juſt opportunity, *viz. By the Pomps and Vanities there are ſeveral things meant, ſome of them ſuch as were u'sd by the Heathens, in ſome unlawful Sports of theirs, wherein we are not now ſo much concern'd, there being none of them remaining among us.*

Well, 'tis a little late now, but I ſhould be glad to meet you here ſome other Night to talk of Matters of the Theatre. Here boy, receive your Reckoning,— Friend *Johnſon*, I thank you for bringing me to a Bottle of good Wine.

Stay,

Stay, I proteſt I had almoſt forgot : I have a Paper in my Pocket concerning the Stage, and 'twas given me this Morning by a young Lady——

Johnſ. I am afraid you have quite forgot, are you ſure it was a young Lady ? Ha, Mr. *Smith* ; perhaps this is like my Friend *Will*'s old Woman.

Smith. My young Lady like your Friend's old Woman ! I aſſure you Sir you are miſtaken, She's in her bloom of Beauty as well as Wit, and that the latter flouriſhes in her, you ſhall ſee immediately, She's a little brief, I muſt confeſs ; her writing is like her ſelf ; the Poſſeſſion and Enjoyment of either, would but raiſe our Wiſhes and deſires, for new fruition.

F 4. *Johnſ.*

Johnſ. Prithee, let me ſee this ſo celebrated Offspring of a Beauty——— you uſe me as a Jilt does a preſſing Lover; you raiſe me to a height of expectation which I can't bear, till at laſt my deſires fly out, and the fruition's loſt.

Smith. You know Ceremony is always us'd to Ladies ; but not to keep you longing, here 'tis ; read it, and give me your opinion.

A

A Short

ESSAY

ON THE

STAGE.

*TOtus Mundus agit Hi-
ftrionem,* is a Saying
demonftratively true : All
Mankind are Actors; tho'
the Lives of fome pafs a-
way

way in gawdy Show and
Opera, and the Lives of
others are fhuffl'd over, and
fpent in wild Confufion;
like irregular Plays, whofe
Scenes are ill, and often
fhifted: And tho' in reali-
ty, we, (even while we are
Spectators in a Theatre)
play and act the Droll, or
ferious parts of our Lives,
our felves; yet are we pleas'd
with the Reprefentation
there, as we are, when we
fee our Faces in a Glafs.
Every Spectator, *Narciffus-*
like, may view his Sha-
dow in this Well, and fall
in

in Love with the Phantom
if he pleases.

The use of the Stage, is
to Instruct and Delight, and
where the Representation
fails in either of these Points,
it fails of the end; for Instruction (in a Theatre particularly) without Pleasure,
is as heavy, as Pleasure without Instruction, is light.

Instruction like a Plant,
may shoot forth into many
branches, but at best, they
would look bare and na-
ked, without the flourish-
ing Ornament of blooming
Leaves; for, 'tis through
those

thofe the Reprefentation
courts, and Gently bends to
the applaufe of the Audience,
as fpreading Boughs receive
the Southern Breezes.

Now, on the other hand,
Delight may pleafe or take
the Eye a little while, like
full blown Rofes in a Gar-
den; and while the Actor
gathers them, to ftrew your
Bed of Pleafure, you are ra-
vifh'd with the Odour, but
'foon as e'er you prefs them
for Enjoyment, your De-
light is Crufh'd.

The Reprefentation then
ought to appear like the
Orange-

Orange-Tree, with Bloſſoms, to pleaſe the View, and Fruit to feed on: So that it may be ſuppos'd the Inſtruction ought to proceed from the Delight; (or appear at leaſt to do ſo.) For, the Spectators muſt needs be tempted with the Fruit, viewing the Beauteous Bloſſoms whence it grew.

I ſhall now look into the Affairs of the *Engliſh Stage*: that, (as a ſtander by, ſeeing all the Miſcarriages of the Game) I may give my Opinion how it ought to be:

be : shewing where the O-
versights are committed, and
how the like may be avoided for the future.

I would by no means
have a Player made a Sha-
rer, for then he grows so
Sawcy immediately, that the
Poet and the Actor tread
the Stage with equal Foot;
nay, and the Actor in a little while, shall Ten to One,
pretend to turn Poet too.
Actors should indeed ne-
ver have more Sense than
generally they have; a
Parrot-like sort of Cant,
so they can but change
their

their Tone, is fufficient for
them.

The chief Manager, or
Patentee, befides Honefty,
ought at leaft to have a
good fhare of Senfe, if not
fome acquaintance with the
Mufes. However it may
happen that a Patentee has
not a Palate to relifh *Helicon* ; but then 'tis abfolutely
neceffary that fuch a one
fhould keep a Tafter; he
fhould employ and encou-
rage fome induftrious Inha-
bitant of *Parnaffus*, and
make him his Agent to fet
the Playhoufe Leafes; by
                    this

this Method, tho' the Te-
nant Poets take them but
for the term of three, or
six Nights at most; if they
are Substantial Men, they
may be encourag'd often to
renew; and the Landlord
have his Rents come in,
with all the Duties.

I would not have the top
Actor a Mad-man, nor be
admir'd for the Rant, and
Clap'd more for his Lungs
than his Action. I would
have all Actresses oblig'd
by their Articles, to a con-
siderable Forfeiture, upon
proof of the abuse of their
Vertue,

Vertue, or rather be Ex-
pell'd the Theatre; for I
think no Woman, after she
has play'd the Whore no-
toriously, can be fancifully
receiv'd upon the Stage for
a Heroine.

I wou'd have a moderate
share of the Gains of the
Theatre, set apart to some
good Use, by publick Or-
der; and special care taken
for the performance of it :
If I may give my Opini-
on, it should be to ease the
Common-wealth of some of
its useless Members, either
by maintaining Old Decre-

G   pid

pid Perſons, or putting a
ſelect number of poor Chil-
dren Apprentices Yearly,
to ſome honeſt and uſeful
Employments; and all Play-
ers ſhou'd be oblig'd to
contribute a certain *Quan-
tum* out of every Pound they
gain, towards it. This wou'd
ſeem as it were a kind of
Compenſation for the Idle-
neſs of their own Lives;
'twoud look like a Purchaſe
upon their Country, and
be a ſort of buying their
way of Living.

I

I wou'd have Seats fepa-
rately for the Men and
Women; which wou'd per-
haps be the beft Method
to leffen the company of
the Masks and Vizards in
the Pit, who beftow their
Half-crown only to make
Prize of fome unwary Gen-
tleman, whom they may
Cully out of a more cor-
fiderable Sum; and be a
very effectual means to hinder the difmal Confequen-
ces that too often attend
thofe unhappy Encounters.

This feparation of the
G 2   Sexes,

Sexes, wou'd cut off all conveniencies and opportunities for such sort of Engagements, or however, it must be granted, it wou'd totally take away the strongest and most powerful parts of the Temptation: It wou'd secure the Ladies from the foolish and vexatious Impertinencies of the Fluttering Fops, and protect them from their Noise and Nonsense; the Moral of the *Drama* wou'd be consequently more minded, and the Poet's Sense and Player's Action more regarded: Bad

Poets

Poets cou'd never be able then to pass such Stuff on the Audience, as they daily do; and even the Best would be oblig'd to a greater care and pains in their Productions.

By this nice attention and regard to the Performance, we shou'd have fewer Plays, yet more good ones. The number of our Dishes wou'd be lessen'd, but the remaining few, wou'd be more Wholsom and Palatable.

I wou'd have such *Immorality* and *Prophaneness* as the

the Master of the *Revels*
Marks to be cut out, abfolutely refus'd the Stage, and
a nice care taken that nothing pafs to compliment
Vice, or difcourage Ver-
tue : Nothing that bears
the leaft tendency to Immo-
defty, fhou'd be permitted.
By this means, the Ladies
might came boldly to a new
Play; and not be at the
trouble of enquiring into its
Character, before tthey appear at the Performance:
They need not then be a-
fraid of paying too dear for
their Divrefion, nor of being

ing at the coft of Blufhes
as well as Mony, for their
Entertainment.

The Stage being thus re-
gulated, it will afford us In-
ftruction as well as Delight,
or at leaft it will become an
Innocent Diverfion : And
in order to encourage it's
continuance in this State, I
wou'd have all Ladies, (as
I wou'd my felf) come con-
ftantly on the P O E T's
Night

Mr. *Johnf.*

Mr. *Johns.* Well, all I have to say, Mr. *Smith*, is, 'tis a Lady's you tell me; I am a Lady's humble Servant at all times.

Mr. *Smith.* And I am yours Sir; come, will you walk Mr. *Johnson*?

Johns. O Sir,——nay, but pray now,——

Smith. Indeed Sir,—— I won't take the Wall of you by no means,—— you are Sir *Jeremy Congreve's* Back,——- pray Sir,—— Your most Humble Servant.

———————

F I N I S.